FAR-OUT and UNUSUAL pets

Tarantulas
Cool Pets!

Enslow Elementary
an imprint of

E ‖ **Enslow Publishers, Inc.**
40 Industrial Road
Box 398
Berkeley Heights, NJ 07922
USA

http://www.enslow.com

Alvin and Virginia
Silverstein and Laura
Silverstein Nunn

Enslow Elementary, an imprint of Enslow Publishers, Inc.

Enslow Elementary® is a registered trademark of Enslow Publishers, Inc.

Library of Congress Cataloging-in-Publication Data

Silverstein, Alvin.
  Tarantulas : cool pets! / by Alvin Silverstein, Virginia Silverstein and Laura Silverstein Nunn.
     p. cm. — (Far-out and unusual pets)
  Includes index.
  Summary: "Provides basic information about tarantulas and keeping them as pets"—Provided by
publisher.
  ISBN 978-0-7660-3883-7
  1. Tarantulas as pets—Juvenile literature. I. Silverstein, Virginia B. II. Nunn, Laura Silverstein.
III. Title.
  SF459.T37S55 2011
  639'.7—dc22
                                        2010054005
Future editions:
Paperback ISBN 978-1-4644-0128-2
ePUB ISBN 978-1-4645-1035-9
PDF ISBN 978-1-4646-1035-6

Printed in the United States of America
012012 The HF Group, North Manchester, IN
10 9 8 7 6 5 4 3 2 1

To Our Readers: We have done our best to make sure all Internet Addresses in this book were
active and appropriate when we went to press. However, the author and the publisher have no
control over and assume no liability for the material available on those Internet sites or on other Web
sites they may link to. Any comments or suggestions can be sent by e-mail to comments@enslow.com
or to the address on the back cover.

Photo Credits: AP Images/Bullit Marquez, p. 7; © iStockphoto.com/Daniel Laflor, p. 9;
Minden Pictures/Mark Moffett, p. 43; Photo by Dr. Byunghwan Lim, p. 36; Photo Researchers, Inc.:
© Gustoimages, p. 44, © John Mitchell, p. 16; Photograph by Richard Gallon, courtesy of the British
Tarantula Society, p. 21; Rick C. West, pp. 12, 13, 14, 20; Shutterstock.com, pp. 1, 3, 4, 8, 11,
19, 22, 26, 29, 31; © Wegner/ARCO/naturepl, pp. 40–41; www.roamingcattle.com/tarantula,
p. 32.

Illustration Credits: Gerald Kelley (www.geraldkelley.com)

Cover Photo: Shutterstock.com

Contents

1

Eek! Big Hairy Spiders!

What do you do when you spot a spider in your house? Do you get scared? If you do, you can admit it. Lots of people freak out at just the sight of a tiny spider. It seems kind of funny that many people are afraid of spiders. We are so much bigger than they are!

But what if the spider wasn't so little? How would you feel if it were almost the size of a rat? And hairy! Would you want to make a quick getaway? Or would you be curious and want to

Aren't Tarantulas Dangerous?

Not to people. Their bite might hurt, but it won't kill you.

Tarantulas got their bad reputation hundreds of years ago. It started in Taranto, Italy, where they also got their name. People believed that these big spiders caused a terrible illness. Supposedly, this illness could be cured only by dancing a fast dance called a tarantella. We know now that the people were probably bitten by a different kind of spider. (And dancing didn't help!)

check it out? If you're not afraid of big, hairy spiders, you might like a tarantula for a pet.

Tarantulas are the world's largest spiders. It is easy to understand why a lot of people think they are creepy looking. After all, they have a big, plump, hairy body and eight long, hairy legs. They look sneaky as they move along slowly. They seem like they are about to pounce on you. But tarantulas are actually gentle animals. They rarely bite unless they get scared. Yes, they are more afraid of you than you are of them!

Tarantulas are gentle animals.

A tarantula has a hairy body and eight legs.

You can learn a lot by observing your pet tarantula.

Tarantulas have been popular pets for many years. Pet owners say that these big spiders make great pets. They are fun and interesting. Just owning one can change a person's mind about its scary reputation. And they are a lot easier to take care of than a dog or even a hamster. They don't make a mess. They don't need a lot of attention, either.

What makes tarantulas so special? Read on to find out why these spiders are such far-out and unusual pets.

2

Wild About Tarantulas

You want a *what* for a pet? Say you want a pet tarantula, and people think you're crazy. Most people don't like the thought of spiders crawling around *inside* their homes. So you can see why someone might not understand your wanting to keep one as a pet.

Tarantulas are not just ordinary spiders, though. They are unusual and fascinating. What better way to learn about them than to watch one up close in your own home? Every day, you can see how your pet spends its time. Watch it dig in the soil, hide out, and eat its food.

Even though a pet tarantula does not live in the wild, it still has its wild ways. Seeing how the tarantula acts in your home can give you an idea of how it would live in the wild.

Tarantulas in the Wild

Tarantulas live mainly in warm places. They may be found in the southwestern United States, Mexico, Central and South America, Africa, Asia, Europe, and Australia. There are more than nine

This female goliath tarantula sits next to its rain
forest burrow in French Guiana.

hundred kinds of tarantulas. Most of them live in underground burrows. However, some types live on the ground or in trees.

Like all spiders, tarantulas make silk. They make it themselves inside their bodies. They actually squirt it out of their rear end! It comes out as a liquid but quickly hardens into silk.

A tarantula makes silk inside its body and squirts it out its back end.

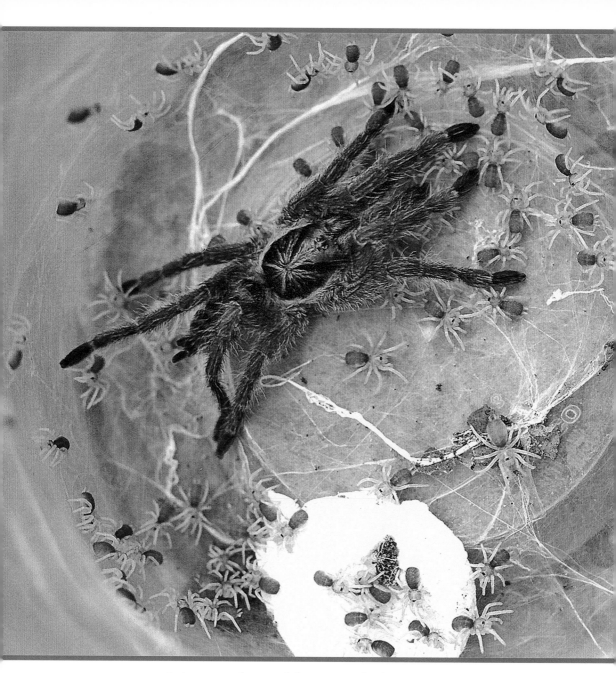

A tarantula and her newly hatched babies

Tarantulas use their silk for many things. For example, a female wraps her eggs in a silk bag, or egg sac. She may lay hundreds of eggs at one time. She will guard the egg sac for many weeks until the baby spiders are ready to hatch.

Tarantulas that live in trees build shelters out of silk. They can rest and hide out there. Some tree tarantulas line a crack in the bark with silk. Their home is like a burrow up in a tree.

Many tarantulas that live in burrows in the ground line their homes with silk. They also use silk when they are hunting. Silky threads stretch out along the ground from the opening of their burrow. The spider can wait for its prey inside its burrow. When an insect or frog touches the silk threads, the tarantula pops out of its burrow. It runs a few steps and sinks its sharp fangs into its prey. The fangs inject a dose of venom (poison). The venom paralyzes its prey. The animal cannot move. Now it is completely weak and helpless. The tarantula may eat its meal right away or wrap

The Little Giant

The world's largest tarantula can be found in South America. That would be the goliath tarantula. This little giant may have a 3.5-inch (9-cm) body and a leg span of 10 inches (25 cm). It is commonly called the bird-eating spider because it has been known to eat birds.

it up in silk and save it for later. These spiders can go for a long time without food—for many weeks or even months!

Tarantulas Up Close

A tarantula is known for its large size. The average tarantula has a 2-inch (5-cm) body and a leg span of 4 to 5 inches (10 to 13 cm). Compare that to the average house spider that is less than an inch long, including its legs! Tarantulas can be more than ten times the size of a house spider.

Far Out!

Soup for Spiders

Most tarantulas eat mainly insects, such as crickets and moths. Some bigger tarantulas may also eat small mice, frogs, lizards, and even birds. Like other spiders, tarantulas cannot eat their prey whole. A spider's venom does more than paralyze its prey. It turns the insect's insides into a soupy liquid. When the spider is ready to eat, it sucks up its meal using strawlike mouthparts. Soup, anyone?

Tarantulas are also known for their hairy bodies and legs. The hairs are not soft, but rather prickly. Tarantulas that live in North and South America use their prickly hairs to defend themselves. The spider will kick or fling these hairs if it is scared or annoyed. (It uses its body hairs as a weapon, much as a porcupine does with its quills.) The hairs have a chemical in them that will cause an itchy rash when they sink into an enemy's skin.

Tarantulas from Australia, Europe, Asia, and Africa have shorter body hairs. They don't flick their hairs like other tarantulas do. Instead, they defend themselves by biting with their poison fangs. These are not the kind of spiders that people keep as pets. They get nervous and annoyed very easily.

If you look at a tarantula closely, you can see its eyes on top of its head. But it doesn't have just two eyes. There are eight of them! That doesn't mean it can see better, though. In fact, a tarantula

A tarantula is covered in prickly hairs.

can't see very well at all. It depends more on touch, taste, and smell to learn about its world. It doesn't have a nose, but it can sense chemicals in the air with special organs on its feet. And it can "taste" the air with the hairs on its legs and mouth.

Lose Any Body Parts?

A tarantula may lose a leg trying to escape an enemy. Luckily, the leg will grow back when the tarantula molts, or sheds its skin. It will be smaller than the others for a while, though. It will take several molts to get the leg back to its normal size.

Far Out!

Growing Up

A tarantula's skin doesn't stretch like a person's does. Spiders have a hard outer covering, called an exoskeleton. When the tarantula grows, its exoskeleton gets too tight for its body. It has to shed its outer covering in a process called molting. Underneath is a fresh new covering that gives the spider more room to grow.

Even though a tarantula has eight eyes, it cannot see very well.

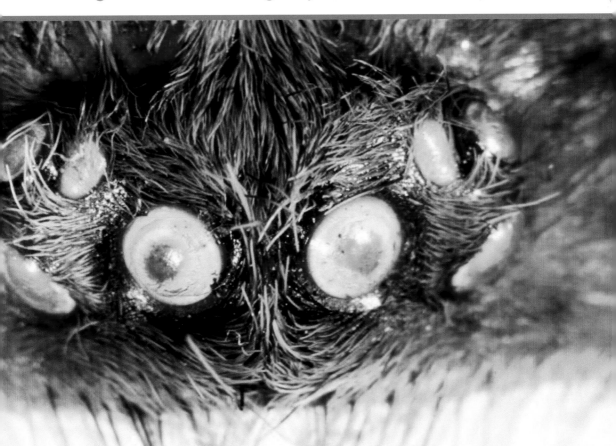

Far Out!

Are Tarantulas Insects?

Spiders are often called insects. Sure, they are all creepy crawlies. But spiders are *not* insects. They actually belong to a different group of animals, called arachnids.

What's the difference between insects and arachnids? For one thing, insects have three body parts. Spiders have two. Another difference is that insects have six legs. Spiders have eight! Spiders also don't have any wings, as some insects do. They don't have antennae, either.

All tarantulas have to molt as they grow. Young tarantulas grow quickly. They may molt a dozen or more times during their first year. When they become adults, they molt less often. Adults may molt only once or twice a year.

The best way to get to know a tarantula better is to own one. Are you up for it?

3

Is a Tarantula Right for You?

Thinking about getting a tarantula for a pet? Know what you are getting into first. Tarantulas may look fuzzy, but they are not soft and cuddly like a cat. And you cannot teach one to come when you call it like you can a dog. (If you can figure out how to teach your pet tarantula to do tricks, *that* would be a neat trick!) Actually, the fact that tarantulas are so different and unusual is what makes them such cool pets.

Killer Spiders?

Scared of the big, hairy spider? You can probably blame
television, movies, and books for that. For years, we have
been taught that tarantulas are dangerous killer spiders.
They will attack you when given the chance. That may
make for a good scary movie, but that is not fair to these
poor, misunderstood spiders. In reality, a tarantula would
rather run and hide than attack a person.

Getting Your Very Own Tarantula

With more than nine hundred kinds of tarantulas, which one would make a good pet? Not all tarantulas can be kept as pets. Some are more active than others. Some get very nervous and are more likely to bite when handled. Tarantulas that make good pets are ones that are gentle and laid-back. They don't get upset easily.

The Chilean rose tarantula is one of the most popular pet varieties.

Male or Female?

It is best to stick with a female tarantula. Adult males do not make very good pets. They are much more active than females. Males also don't live long after they reach adult size. You may have them for only six months to a year. But females can live for a very long time, usually fifteen to twenty years!

Some of the most popular ones include the desert blond, the Chilean rose, the Costa Rican zebra, and the pinktoe tarantula. It is a good idea to research these tarantulas before you buy one.

When you're ready for your own tarantula, where do you get one? It's never a good idea to pick one out of the wild. It might not be the kind of tarantula you want to keep as a pet. It could get upset easily. It won't be used to being around people.

A good place to get a tarantula is from a breeder. Breeders usually take special care of their animals. Often they have raised the tarantulas they sell from tiny baby spiders. Breeders can also answer any questions you might have about tarantulas. They can give you information about their backgrounds, as well.

Many pet stores also sell tarantulas. But a pet store is not a good place to get one. Workers may not know a lot about the animals they sell. And they probably know very little about their background. Most of the tarantulas sold in pet stores were caught in the wild.

How Many Tarantulas?

In the wild, tarantulas may be found alone or in groups. The groups may be small, with just two or three spiders. Or there may be dozens of them living in the same area. However, these groups are not close-knit families like ants or termites. Most

In the wild, tarantulas may live alone or in a group.

tarantulas are likely to eat their "family members," if given the chance.

Tarantulas are rather shy animals. They rarely leave their burrows to hang out with their neighbors. They usually don't go farther than a few inches from their underground home.

So if you don't want your tarantulas snacking on one another, it's probably a good idea to keep just one. If you would like more than one, you must keep them in separate homes.

Handle With Care

Some people say pet owners should not handle tarantulas at all. People are more likely to hurt the spider than the other way around. Even a short fall can hurt or kill your spider.

If you really want to handle your tarantula, you need to be super careful. Make sure you don't hold it high above the floor. It would be better to handle the spider above something soft, such as a pillow or bed. That way it won't get hurt if it falls.

Most experts agree that it
is best not to handle your
tarantula. If you do pick
up your pet, hold it over a
pillow or bed. If it falls,
it will not get hurt.

Tarantulas have two fangs.

Try This!

Want to know a safe way to pick up your tarantula without hurting the spider or yourself? Try this! Scoop up the tarantula with a plastic cup. This works well if you need to remove the spider to clean out its tank. It's also a good way to capture your tarantula if it escapes and you need to get it back.

In general, tarantulas are not crazy about being handled. They may become nervous. You need to be gentle. If you handle a tarantula roughly, it will flick its hairs. If any hairs get stuck in your skin, they will cause a reaction. Your skin will become red, swollen, and itchy. And if you get one of these hairs in your eyes it will feel even worse! Always wash your hands after touching a tarantula. It is a good idea to wear protective glasses, too.

Pet tarantulas usually don't bite. But they may grab hold of your finger with their fangs if they are in danger of falling. Tarantula bites are generally not dangerous. You won't need to go to the emergency room. But they may cause allergic reactions in some people.

4

A Home for Your Tarantula

No one likes spiders crawling freely around the house. And that includes pet ones! Pet tarantulas should be kept in a tank. A small fish tank is fine. Even better are the plastic tanks called "kritter keepers." Luckily, unlike most pets, tarantulas don't need a lot of room. Even in the wild, they hardly ever leave their underground home. And when they do, they don't go far. When you set up your tarantula's new home, make sure it is a lot like its living conditions in nature.

A plastic tank makes a great home for your pet tarantula. It does not need to be large. Tarantulas do not move far from their burrow.

All the Comforts of Home

A tarantula's tank should be tightly covered by a mesh lid. The spider's legs have tiny claws on the tips that help it hold onto surfaces so it can easily climb things. Your tarantula will climb the walls of its tank. So make sure the lid is always tightly in place. If given the chance, the tarantula will escape. Your family would not be very happy about finding a big hairy spider in their beds!

Cover the bottom of the tank with 2 to 3 inches (5 to 8 cm) of potting soil. Make sure there are places for the tarantula to hide under, such as a turned-over, broken plant pot. Your pet may also dig in the soil, making an underground home like it would in the wild. It may stay there most of the time, coming out once in a while.

The tarantula's home should be kept at a warm temperature, between 70 to 80 degrees Fahrenheit (21 to 27 degrees Celsius). Remember, tarantulas live in warm places in the wild. You can keep a heating pad under the tank. But don't let the temperature get too warm. In the wild, tarantulas spend a lot of time on the ground, where it is cooler. If they get overheated, they could dry out and die. So keep the tank out of direct sunlight.

Who's Hungry?

Looking at its size, you might think a tarantula eats a lot. Actually, tarantulas are not big eaters at all. They can go for long periods without food.

What do they usually eat? Live crickets are a popular choice for pet tarantulas. (You can buy the crickets in a pet store.) Most tarantulas can survive on just one or two crickets a week. Larger tarantulas may eat up to six crickets a week.

You don't have to worry about your tarantula eating too much. If it's not hungry, it won't even bother with a cricket leaping by. However, it might catch its prey, wrap it in silk, and save it for later.

Far Out!

Tank for Your Tarantula

Unless your pet tarantula is super-sized, do not get a tank larger than ten gallons. There are some good reasons for that. For one thing, it is a waste of space. In a larger cage, the tarantula will seem "lost" with the extra floor space. It may start pacing back and forth endlessly, looking for "home." And the spider's food—often live crickets—might starve to death before the tarantula finds it in an overly big home.

This tarantula is eating a grasshopper.

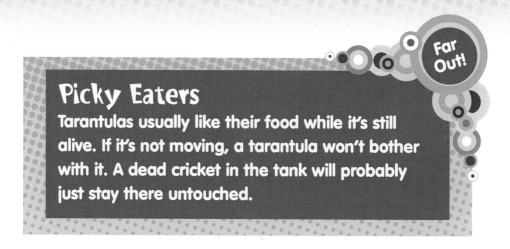

Picky Eaters

Tarantulas usually like their food while it's still alive. If it's not moving, a tarantula won't bother with it. A dead cricket in the tank will probably just stay there untouched.

But if the cricket is still hopping around the next morning, it is always a good idea to remove it. You don't want it to annoy the tarantula, especially if your pet is molting.

Tarantulas need to have water every day. Keep a shallow water bowl in the tank for drinking. It is a good idea to put some pebbles in the bowl. That way if a cricket jumps in, it won't drown.

Leave Me Alone, I'm Molting

If you notice your tarantula lying on its back and looking kind of dead, don't worry. It is probably just getting ready to molt.

How can you tell that your tarantula is getting ready to molt? For a couple of weeks before molting, your spider will likely refuse to eat. It may rest on a "bed" of silk. The spider may also lose hairs on its abdomen, leaving a bald spot.

When the tarantula is ready to molt, it will flip onto its back. Its legs will stick out into the air, or off to the side. It may look like it's dead, but it's not. (A dying tarantula doesn't turn over that way. It usually curls its legs under itself.)

This tarantula just molted. Its old exoskeleton is on the left.

Handle your pet tarantula with care.

Molting can take anywhere from fifteen minutes to several hours. Once the tarantula sheds its exoskeleton, its body will be very soft and tender. It is very important that you don't bother the spider while it is molting. It is very weak and helpless during this time and can die if it is disturbed. It may take several days to weeks for the new exoskeleton to harden. The spider may not be up to eating for several days after molting. You should wait a week or two before giving it any food. By then it should be acting "normal" again.

Have you changed your mind about tarantulas? Do they still give you the creeps? Or are they cooler than you thought? If you want to keep one as a pet, learn everything you can about it first. This is a pet you may have for a long time—for up to twenty years!

Words to Know

abdomen—The hind part of an animal's body.

antennae—Feelers; a pair of movable organs on the head of some insects; typically used for smell and taste.

breeder—A person who cares for animals and raises their babies.

exoskeleton—The hard outer shell or covering of many animals.

molt—The shedding of an animal's hair, skin, or feathers, which later grow back.

prey—An animal that is hunted and eaten by predators.

venom—Poison produced by animals such as snakes, insects, and spiders.

Learn More

Books

Breene, Robert G. *Quick & Easy Tarantula Care.* Neptune City, N.J.: T.F.H. Publications, Inc., 2005.

Leavitt, Amie Jane. *Care for a Pet Tarantula.* Hockessin, Del.: Mitchell Lane Publishers, 2008.

Schultz, Stanley A., and Marguerite J. Schultz. *The Tarantula Keeper's Guide.* Hauppauge, N.Y.: Barron's Educational Series, Inc., 2009.

Walls, Jerry G. *Tarantulas.* Irvine, Calif.: Advanced Vivarium Systems, 2005.

Web Sites

"American Tarantula Society Headquarters"

<http://www.atshq.org/>

"The Web Home for Tarantula Keepers"

<http://tarantulas.com>

Index